America
the
Grammar

Improve Your Communication
In Any Situation

M. A. CUMMINGS

ISBN 979-8-88832-900-9 (paperback)
ISBN 979-8-88832-901-6 (digital)

Copyright © 2024 by M. A. Cummings

All rights reserved. No part of this publication may be reproduced, distributed, or transmitted in any form or by any means, including photocopying, recording, or other electronic or mechanical methods without the prior written permission of the publisher. For permission requests, solicit the publisher via the address below.

Christian Faith Publishing
832 Park Avenue
Meadville, PA 16335
www.christianfaithpublishing.com

Printed in the United States of America

To Megan, for your undying but inexplicable faith.
To Ava, Molly, and Rachel, for serving as motivation.
I am blessed beyond measure for each of you.

Contents

1. Introduction: Why?..vii
   You're Serious. A Grammar Book?
2. On Writing Well 1
   It's Not What You Think
3. The Eight Parts of Speech 5
4. Common Errors and Easy Ways to Fix Them 8
5. References 47

Introduction: Why?

You're Serious. A Grammar Book?

A book on grammar? How hard does falling asleep have to be?

Of the material you could be reading, a book on grammar—even the one you are holding now, pulsating with excitement—probably ranks on your interest scale somewhere near irrigation advances during the ninth century and precolonial botany.

Stay with me, though, because I have solid reasons why good grammar plays a vital role in succeeding in life.

First, what is *grammar*?

Using a search engine, you may find something like this from the Oxford reference: "the whole system and structure of a language or of languages in general, usually taken as consisting of syntax and morphology (including inflections) and sometimes also phonology and semantics."

That doesn't help.

How about Wikipedia?

1. The study of a language: how it works and everything about it. This is background research on language.
2. The study of sentence structure. Rules and examples show how the language should be used. This is a correct usage grammar, as in a textbook or manual/guide.
3. The system that people learn as they grow up. This is the native speaker's grammar.

Not bad, but it needs simplification. This is my definition:

> Grammar: the widely accepted rules of a given language that promote accurate communication

You do not have to endure a grammar class to know when someone is breaking English grammar rules. Most of the time, you know it when you hear it.

What I am going to do with this book is help you when *you are the one breaking the rules.*

Why should you care?

Tell me if you have said or heard something like this: *Who cares about grammar, usage, or punctuation? The only thing that matters is the people I'm communicating with understand what I'm saying.*

It's a strong argument, and not long ago I said the same.

Here's why: good or bad, communication has consequences.

I repeat, <u>communication has consequences</u>.

Let's say you and I are facing each other from opposite sides of a wide country road. I need you to come over to my side. But you are deaf, so I have to use hand gestures.

If I use the correct hand gestures and you move in my direction, I have communicated properly. If after seeing those gestures you walk in a different direction or stand still, I haven't.

Fairly simple.

What if we are no longer standing on a wide country road but a busy highway at rush hour on a Friday evening? Also, what if you are blindfolded and your legs are tied together?

The concept is the same—I want you to come over to my side—but because of the additional details, getting you across is more challenging. Unless I want you to decorate the front end of a truck, I better communicate with you carefully.

AMERICA THE GRAMMAR

How about this text, girlfriend to a boyfriend?

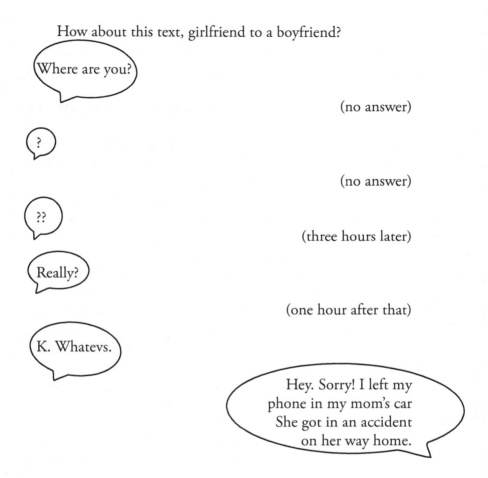

When we see the whole picture, we learn the truth.

When delivering information from one point to another, the smallest detail surrounding the sender, receiver, purpose, and medium can change how a message is interpreted—sometimes wildly.

Communication and first impressions

First impressions happen quickly, and they last a long time. These are the two main conclusions drawn from multiple studies about first impressions.

A 2014 study by a professor at the University of Glasgow showed when a group of test subjects heard someone only say the word "Hello," they were able to form consistent opinions about that person *in less than one second.*

Whether it's the spoken or electronic word, a first impression is always made.

More bad news: the same study indicates that a first impression from an *online interaction* (e.g., posted photo or video, text, etc.) is more often negative versus when two people meet in person, face to face.

Since much of our interaction and communication with people is via the written word online, we must ensure we communicate properly to make and maintain a good impression.

Here is the good news: good grammar is not difficult.

Let's say your school announces the formation of a special team. Once members earn their spot on the roster, for the rest of their lives, they will be considered intelligent and high class. They will have privileges and honors bestowed on them just for being part of this team. They will earn the attention of the opposite sex and have high-quality friends and good-paying jobs. On social media, if it interests them, they will be followed, liked, and quoted more than those outside of this team. And no matter what any of them does, they will always be a part of this group, never to be removed.

This team exists. Membership is open to all willing to put forth no more effort than that of any math, language, drama, music, or sports club.

To be part of this team, there is one requirement: you must communicate properly.

If you're still with me, good. When we're done, you will have the baseline grammar and communication skills you need.

Remember, communication—good or bad—has consequences.

Why you should listen to me

Are you naturally good at something like sports, video games, fashion, or music?

AMERICA THE GRAMMAR

When it comes to skills in life, I'm average at a lot of things. One subject I was inherently good at, however, was grammar. In Mr. Miller's and Mrs. Quaintance's grammar classes where we diagrammed sentences until we drew blood—only a slight exaggeration—and achieved platinum-level grammar skills, I didn't struggle much. Since then, I achieved a master's in rhetoric and composition from Northern Arizona University, have written columns for two university newspapers, wrote grammar and movie review columns for a 1,500-employee company and position pieces for two, national election campaigns, and served as a regular columnist for two websites.

I write a lot, and I know grammar.

Grammar isn't difficult if you look at it the right way. Good grammar is about producing a thought that is properly transferred to your audience. When you are doing it well, you don't notice, and only here and there do you have to make adjustments to stay on course.

Work with me, and you will produce that flow.

This book is for you

America the Grammar is intended for traditional and homeschool students in grades 7–12. However, this book will help any reader improve his/her communication—graduate school, company employees and management, or stay-at-home moms and dads.

Why a book, and not just a website?

Am I aware there is this thing called the Internet where I could build a website in fifteen minutes and send the link to everyone? Yes, I am. But for my primary audience, web access isn't always available or consistent. You need this book to be tactile, portable, accessible, and not reliant on electricity.

Last note on the importance of grammar

Life is a game of inches.

If you don't believe me, ask America's Olympic swimmer Jason Lezak. On August 11, 2008, at the Beijing Olympics, Lezak shot ahead of France's Alain Bernard to finish first in the 4x100m freestyle relay in 3:08.24. Bernard finished behind Lezak in 3:08.32, *a mere 0.08 seconds* after Lezak.

Both Lezak and Bernard were stellar athletes. They spent years constructing their bodies, minds, and souls to prepare for those events. Yet it was hardly a fingernail that decided who took the gold. A silver medal is great, but as the saying goes, second place is first loser.

Whatever Lezak did, whatever last twitch of muscle strand that activated to shoot his arm a fraction of an inch forward, whatever "it" may have been was very little, a game of not just inches but, in this case, a fraction of an inch. There are more examples like these than stars in the sky.

Why should communicating properly be any different?

Whether it's a phone call, voicemail, email, text, social media post or video, report, speech before a class, or address before a nation, we need to do better at conveying our message.

Knowing good grammar and usage does not mean you can name all parts of speech at will, nor does it mean correcting everyone you speak with when they make a mistake (not a good way to make friends).

You should care because communicating properly can mean an A over a B or B over C, your boss wondering if he made the right choice in hiring you, or if the law you write as a legislator is properly constructed to serve the American people. Needless conflicts occur when recipients of your messages do not fully comprehend your intended message.

Since life is a game of inches, why not stack as many inches in your favor as possible? Run a bit farther (not *further*) during practice. Try one more equation before a math test. Do a few more sit-ups when you think you are done. Get as much education as you can, formal and informal. Make the extra effort to communicate properly so you have the advantage, because many victories in life are won with the smallest of margins.

Life's inches matter.

On Writing Well

It's Not What You Think

Much emphasis is put on writing well, but more often, instructors and teachers concentrate on style issue (attention-grabbing titles, action verbs, colorful word choices) and not enough on properly getting the message across. There needs to be an effective compromise between proper usage and readability.

How? There are three methods:

1. Be professionally conversational. Write as if you are talking to your audience, but not with your close friends. Bland writing pervades our communication, so if you use an upgraded conversational tone, you will improve your communication.

2. Be straightforward. In writing a school paper, proposal, speech, sales pitch, and darn near every time you are simply passing information to an audience of one or a thousand, use what Aristotle himself called a triptych.

    - Tell them what you're going to tell them.
    - Tell them.
    - Tell them what you told them.

    Various teachers may tell you not to use this approach, accusing it of being stale and lacking the ability to keep your audience's attention. The reason they are wrong is they forget you have a great deal of flexibility in how you deliver those three points. Style is almost always up to you.

3. Take a break. A nearly foolproof way to ensure good writing and avoid catastrophic mistakes is to step away from your writing for at least thirty minutes, come back to it, and read it aloud before you submit. The longer the piece, the longer you should take a break from it. The famous author, Stephen King, could take up to six weeks before reviewing a book before sending it to a publisher. More often than not, we are too close to our work to see mistakes. When you are too far deep into a topic, your brain needs pause and separation. Trust me, coming back to your writing after a break yields tremendous results.

The (other) rhetorical question no one's asking and one you're already answering

Most of you have heard of rhetorical questions, questions whose answers are so obvious they need not be said aloud: *Is the Pope Catholic?*

There is another definition of rhetoric: like the filters you use with a camera lens to see an image better, there are four filters we use to understand a given piece of communication. These filters include the following:

1. Sender
2. Receiver
3. Purpose
4. Medium

An expansion on Aristotle's Rhetorical Triangle, from here on we will call this the rhetorical diamond. The good news is you are already using this diamond in your head. Have you ever switched from text to email or email to phone call? Instead of a written reply to a text, did you send an emoji or GIF? Why did you switch? What thought process occurred between hitting Send and changing it up?

The following are the four points on the rhetorical diamond.

1. Sender
    Who are you? What is your position? Why are you the sender and not someone else?
2. Receiver
    Who is your audience? Why? Should it be someone else?
3. Purpose
    Why are you sending this message? Do you want to inform, convince, persuade, or entertain?
4. Medium
    Text, email, paper, online post or thread, slide presentation, oral presentation, billboard, etc.

By using the diamond—answering the four points before releasing your message—you boost the odds of your message being interpreted as intended.

Each point offers you an option to change how clearly your message is received.

1. Sender
    A parent who tries to tell his child how to throw a football may not have as much success as a football coach.
2. Receiver
    The owner of a company—versus someone who washes the building's windows—receives a customer complaint.
3. Purpose
    Do you want your audience to act on your information or just be informed? Do you want them to laugh, cry, or yawn?
4. Medium
    A text that says "I'm sorry" versus holding a bouquet in front of your audience while taking a knee. Which would have more impact according to your purpose?

All four points are important, but your audience is the most important. In school, you know who your audience usually is: teachers. That is the good news. The bad news is your teachers may be wrong about a given topic, or they could be wrong about grammar, usage, and style. Also, since teachers are human, they might just have a problem with you personally. The rule also does not change if your teacher is Mom, Dad, or a homeschooling parent in a pod.

Write and speak <u>for your audience</u>. Pay attention to how they want homework submitted and how they wish to be communicated with, no matter how wrong you think they are.

The Eight Parts of Speech

English has flaws, the greatest of these is the multitude of exceptions for every rule. However, one of its strengths is the limited number of parts of speech.

1. <u>Noun</u>—person, place, or thing
2. <u>Verb</u>—a word that describes an action, state, or occurrence and forms the main part of the predicate of a sentence
3. <u>Pronoun</u>—a word that can function by itself as a noun phrase and refers either to the participants in the discourse or to someone or something mentioned elsewhere in the discourse
4. <u>Preposition</u>—word governing, and usually preceding, a noun or pronoun and expressing a relation to another word or element in the clause
5. <u>Adjective</u>—word or phrase naming an attribute, added to or grammatically related to a noun to modify or describe it
6. <u>Adverb</u>—word or phrase that modifies or qualifies an adjective, verb, or other adverb or a word group, expressing a relation of place, time, circumstance, manner, cause, degree, etc.
7. <u>Interjection</u>—an abrupt remark, made especially as an aside or interruption
8. <u>Conjunction</u>—word used to connect clauses or sentences or to coordinate words in the same clause (e.g., *and, because, but, yet, or, nor, although, since, unless, while, where,* etc.)

Here is an acronym to help you remember: I-N-P-P-A-V-A-C—I Never Put Pizza And Vegetables Alongside Cake

Punctuation marks

While this is a plus for English for its attempt at simplicity, we use fourteen different punctuation marks. Examples are shown in the "Common Errors and Easy Ways to Fix Them" section.

1. Period—ends a sentence or abbreviates.
2. Question mark—asks a question.
3. Exclamation point—expresses excitement, anger, or alarm.
4. Comma—separates lists or in salutations.
5. Colon—introduces an idea or list.
6. Semicolon—connects independent clauses.
7. Dash—indicates range or connections or an abrupt halt to speech or text.
8. Hyphen (shorter than a dash)—connects two or more words into a compound term.
9. Brackets []—to clarify. If omitted, the sentence makes sense.
10. Braces {}—not usually in written form except for math or coding.
11. Parentheses ()—to add a description or clarify; can often be replaced with commas.
12. Apostrophe—abbreviates or shows possessives and plurals for lowercase letters.
13. Quotation marks—attribute words by another person or indicate questionable quality. Single quotes are for quotes within quotes.
14. Ellipses "…"—three periods together to indicate an omission of text without changing the meaning.

If you think punctuation doesn't matter, consider this actual title from a news story:

Actual title:

"Father-to-be killed in gender reveal party"

AMERICA THE GRAMMAR

What if you omitted the hyphens?

"Father to be killed in gender reveal party"

Both are tragic, but they have wildly different meanings.

Common Errors and Easy Ways to Fix Them

Now you know the theoretical basics of good communication. What follows is the tactical part where I list common errors in English grammar and usage and how to avoid them.

I do not cover every possible rule for every conceivable error and do not list all definitions. You would not read them if I did.

These words and phrases are what I have found to be the most common.

Here we go.

Word/Phrase	Rule	Example
100s (numbers as plurals)	No apostrophe is necessary to make a number plural.	Between the early _1500s and 1800s_, of the 10.7 million Africans taken as slaves, 305,000 of them were brought to the United States.
All of that being said, that being said, that said	No need to remind your audience what you just said. Since most people using this phrase are about to contradict what they just said, use another adverb such as _but_ or _however_.	The Declaration of Independence: "Prudence, indeed, will dictate that Governments long established should not be changed for light and transient causes…" "_But_ when a long train of abuses and usurpations, pursuing invariably the same Object evinces a design to reduce them under absolute Despotism, it is their right, it is their duty, to throw off such Government, and to provide new Guards for their future security."

AMERICA THE GRAMMAR

A/An (adj)	*A* is used before a consonant sound (B, C, D, F, G, H, J, K, L, M, N, P, Q, R, S, T, V, X, Z, and usually W and Y) *An* (adj) is used before a vowel sounding word (A, E, I, O, H, U)	2nd Amendment to the Constitution: "*A* well regulated Militia, being necessary to the security of *a* free State, the right of the people to keep and bear Arms, shall not be infringed." 1st Amendment to the Constitution: "Congress shall make no law respecting *an* establishment of religion, or prohibiting the free exercise thereof."
Accept (v), Except (prep, conj, idiom)	*Accept* (v)—to agree to/with or acknowledge *Except* (prep)—not including, other than. You can generally omit *for* after *except*.	The Serenity Prayer: God, grant me the serenity to *accept* the things I cannot change, the courage to change the things I can, and the wisdom to know the difference. *Except* America, not one country in the world has a constitution that contains "All men are created equal."
Accidently (adv) Accidentally (adv)	Some sources say you can use either, but since *accidentl* is not a word, there seems no reason for *accidently*.	Each of us was not endowed by our Creator *accidentally*; we all have a purpose for being here.
Acerbate (v) Exasperate (v)	*Acerbate* (v)—to agree to/with or acknowledge *Exasperate* (v)—to provoke or infuriate Generally, *acerbate* is making things worse, while *exasperate* is making things more worse, which doesn't make sense. Avoid *acerbate* since it's rare enough that most people will believe you have it wrong.	Do not *exasperate* the problem of big government by voting for more taxes.
Acronyms with Apostrophes (plural, possessive)	Only add an apostrophe with lowercase letters.	Plural: Public education has always been about learning the *ABCs*; however, in the last few decades, the purpose seems to be indoctrination into leftist views. Possessive: The *USA's* number one tourist attraction is liberty.

9

Adverbs	Adverbs modify adjectives or other verbs. They have their purpose, but overall, adverbs are overused. Try an experiment: write how you normally write, and when you review, remove as many adverbs as you can, and see what you think. I am guessing you will see your words will hold greater meaning.	
Affect (v) Effect (n)	*Affect* (v)—to have an effect; make a difference to *Effect* (n)—an event, condition, or state of affairs produced by a cause	The events that occurred on September 11, 2001, will *affect* our country for generations. One way to *affect* an American accent is to speak of freedom and free market principles. The *effect* of faith, hard work, and perseverance is success.
Afterall (adv) After all (adv)	*Afterall* is not a word. *After all* (adv) is correct.	*After all* is said and done, the most happy people are those who choose to be grateful.
Afterward (v) Afterwards (v)	*Afterward* (v) and *Afterwards* (v) are correct but omitting "s" is more formal. Less harm is ever done by going formal, both in speech and choice of clothing	In 1777, the Articles of Confederation and Perpetual Union were created to determine how our government should operate. *Afterward*, because the Articles of Confederation weren't working as well as hoped, the US Constitution was created.
Agnostic (n, adj) Atheist (n)	*Agnostic* (n)—person who doesn't know if there is a God *Agnostic* (adj)—unwilling to commit to an opinion *Atheist* (n)—person who is certain there is not a God	*Atheists* are just angry *agnostics*. She was *agnostic* on whether pineapple should be allowed on pizza.
Ain't	Incorrect contraction for "are not"	Don't do it.
Allude (v) Elude (v)	*Allude* (v)—to refer to something *Elude* (v)—to evade or avoid	A good habit is for lawmakers to *allude* to the constitution daily. One of the worst mistakes you can make is to try to *elude* a police officer.

AMERICA THE GRAMMAR

Allot (v) A lot (adj)	*Alot*—incorrect form of *a lot* *Allot*—to assign or designate a portion	The world's population envies the United States *a lot*. Why do you think so many want to become citizens? The United States *allots* two senators for each state, a total of one hundred.
Already (adv) All ready (adj)	*Already* (adv)—before or by now or the time in question *All ready* (adj)—entirely ready or prepared	We *already* have three ways to change the constitution: the amendment process, a Constitutional Convention, and a Convention of States. We were *all ready* to eat, but Dad stopped us to pray.
Alright (adj, adv, excl) All right (adj)	*All right* (adj)—satisfactory but not especially good; acceptable Though dictionaries say "alright" is becoming acceptable, it is often too informal. "All right" is more appropriate.	At no time in America will everything be *all right* if we don't safeguard our liberties. Matthew McConaughey is known for saying, "All right, all right, all right."
Altogether (adv) All together (adv)	*Altogether* (adv)—completely, all things considered, or on the whole *All together* (adv)—everyone together or everything together	The Articles of Confederation were thrown out *altogether* and replaced with the US Constitution. In America, we stand *all together* or we fall *all together*.
Alumnus (n) Alumna (n) Alumni (n, adj) Alumnae (n, adj)	*Alumnus* (n)—male graduate *Alumna* (n)—female graduate *Alumni* (n)—male graduates *Alumnae* (n)—graduates, mald and female	The *alumnus* appeared at the football game with a painted face, right next to his girlfriend, also an *alumna*, who sported an extremely large foam cowboy hat. They were both cheered by their fellow *alumni* and *alumnae* as they entered the stadium, a few hours before the *alumni* ball.
Ambivalent (adj) Indifferent (adj)	Many confuse *ambivalent* to mean "I don't care either way" when it really means a state of conflicting emotions.	As with nuclear weapons, it's okay to be *ambivalent* about guns. Both can save and take lives.
Amongst (prep) Among (prep)	*Amongst* (prep)—usually a British usage *Among* (prep)—usually an America usage	Declaration of Independence: "We hold these truths to be self-evident, that all men are created equal, that they are endowed by their Creator with certain unalienable Rights, that *among* these are Life, Liberty and the pursuit of Happiness."

Amoral (adj) Immoral (adj)	*Amoral* (adj)—neither moral nor immoral (as in someone not knowing the difference between right and wrong) *Immoral* (adj)—lacking in morality	Rarely will you find an *amoral* person since who doesn't, in their heart, know right from wrong? It is *immoral* to abort a baby.
And/or (conj)	Using *and/or* (conj) can disrupt flow so use either *and* or *or*, not both.	Certain laws can be struck down by lower courts *or* the Supreme Court, depending on the path litigants choose.
Anxious (adj) Eager (adj)	*Anxious* (adj)—usually negative, experiencing worry, unease, or nervousness *Eager* (adj)—usually positive, wanting to do or have something very much	We should be *anxious* about American citizens not being *eager* to learn about our country.
Any more (adv) Anymore (adv)	*Any more* (adv)—determiner, additional in quantity *Anymore* (adv)—lately or no longer	We do not want *any more* people to say "I don't know American history" *anymore*.
Anyway (adv) Anyways (adv) Any way	*Anyway* (adv)—despite the previous statement or regardless *Anyways* (adv)—less formal and one of many words where omitting the "s" at the end is best *Any way*—two words	Despite the Constitution's value in promoting a free and prosperous society, far too many leaders disregard it *anyway*. If there is *any way* to bring down the cost of fuel and ensure we aren't reliant on countries who don't like us, it is to drill and refine in our own country.
Anywhere (adv) Any where	*Anywhere* (adv)—in or to any place *Any where* is incorrect.	While there isn't *anywhere* in the Constitution that gives citizens the right to privacy, various amendments' protections, like the First Amendment, inherently provide for privacy.
Apostrophe (p)	See also "Punctuation Marks" section.	
Ascribe (v) Prescribe (v) Proscribe (v) Subscribe (v)	*Ascribe* (v)—to attribute or credit to *Prescribe* (v)—to advise or authorize use of medical treatment *Proscribe* (v)—to forbid, ban (rarely used) *Subscribe* (v)—to set up to receive regularly, agree with	I *ascribe* the goosebumps I get during the National Anthem to my love of country. He asked his doctor to *prescribe* antibiotics after being stuck for several hours on an airplane.

AMERICA THE GRAMMAR

		Burning the US flag is not *proscribed* by law, but it's not preferred.
		I *subscribe* to Walter E. Williams' and Thomas Sowell's points of view, which is why I *subscribe* to their weekly columns.
As per (prep)	*Per* (prep)—for each is enough	*Per* my voicemail, please see the attached report.
Assure (v) Ensure (v) Insure (v)	*Assure* (v)—to remove doubt, placate *Ensure* (v)—to make certain something will or won't happen *Insure* (v)—protect against a risk, as in car insurance	A strong, American military *assures* the rest of the world that bad guys will be dealt with. It is vital that every generation does what it can to *ensure* our way of life. In the debate of nationalized healthcare, it is nonsensical to compare forcing people to *insure* their car to *insuring* their health.
At all (adv)	*At all* (adv)—under any circumstances. Most of the time, it is unnecessary.	I don't like kale *at all*. versus I don't like kale.
Awake (adj) Awaken (v) Wake (n, v) Woke (v)	*Awake* (adj)—opposite of asleep, alert *Awaken* (v)—to rouse from sleep or evoke a feeling *Wake* (n, v)—a service held for the deceased. To rouse from sleep *Woke* (n)—past tense of *wake*	I was *awake* this morning at 5:00 a.m. Many times, I have *awaken* without an alarm. I will *wake* my little sister up from her nap at 3:00 p.m. Today, we held a *wake* for my grandfather who passed away. Social media is full of people urging others to *wake* up. Yesterday, I *woke* after 10:00 a.m.
Ax (n, v) Axe (n, v)	*Ax* (n, v)—instrument used to cut or chop *Axe* (n, v)—the act of cutting or chopping. *Axe* is more common	The story of George Washington chopping down the cherry tree with an *axe* is not true; it was meant to show Washington's honesty.

		We should _axe_ the 17th Amendment and return choosing US Senators back to state legislatures.
Back in time (adv) Forward in time (adv) Up in time (adv)	The context will determine the meaning, but generally, _time_ is assumed when discussing a timeline.	Ronald Reagan's speech in 1961 warned that there may be a time when we _think back_ when men were free.
Bald-faced (adj) Bold-faced (adj) Boldface (adj)	Both are used but _bald-faced_ (adj) is preferred in edited text. _Boldface_ (adj) also refers to the emphasis (darker, thicker color) put on fonts.	This book is my _bald-faced_ assertion that proper grammar and usage matter. Before our abrupt withdrawal from Vietnam, to say America was losing the war is a _bald-faced_ lie. The teacher criticized Tommy for using too much _boldface_ in his papers.
Bare (adj, v) Bear (n, v)	_Bare_ (adj)— without appropriate covering _Bare_ (v)—uncover, expose _Bear_ (n)—large animal that eats plants, fish, and, occasionally, people _Bear_ (v)—carry, hold, tolerate, maintain direction	If you find yourself walking in the sand, _bare_ your feet so you have _bare_ feet to feel the sand. Unfortunately, many of us must _bear_ the burden of fighting those who seek to fundamentally transform America. The delivery driver was told to _bear_ right. 2nd Amendment: A well-regulated Militia, being necessary to the security of a free State, the right of the people to keep and _bear_ arms, shall not be infringed. Do not feed wild _bears_.
Borrow (v)	_Borrow_ (v)—to receive something with the intention of returning or paying back.	People who _borrow_ more than they can afford risk financial hardship.
Bring (v) Take (v)	_Bring_ (v)—movement toward you _Take_ (v)—movement to anywhere but where you are	_Bring_ (me) pizza. When you go out in the woods, at a minimum, _take_ the following: water, plenty of clothing, and three ways to make a fire.

AMERICA THE GRAMMAR

Cannot (v) Can not	*Cannot* (v) is correct.	We *cannot* let America fall, for if we do, the entire world will enter years of darkness.
Capital (adj, n) Capitol (n)	*Capital* (adj)—single city in each state or country where government is conducted. *Capital* (n)—money or property *Capital* (n)—the death penalty *Capitol* (n)—actual building where government is conducted	Pierre is the *capital* of South Dakota. You would be surprised at how little *capital* you need to start your own business. Assassinating the president of the United States is worthy of *capital* punishment. Members of Congress met in the *Capitol* to announce the new 10 percent flat tax.
Couldn't care less Could care less	If you *could care* less, it means you care a little. If you *could not* care less, you don't care at all.	Many successful people *couldn't care* less what others thought of them.
Cement (n, v) Concrete (adj, n)	*Cement* (n)—one of many ingredients that, when mixed, turns into *concrete* (n), the hardened product. *Cement* (v)—to bond or unite *Concrete* (adj)—specific, real-life, clear	We mixed water with the *cement* to make *concrete*. The 1969 Lunar Module landing is a *concrete* example of American ingenuity.
Church (adj, n) church (n)	Capitalize *Church* when referring to a specific church or denomination by name. *The Church* can also mean the Vatican. Lowercase *church*—a place of worship	Sunday school is often called *church* school. My wife and I were married at St. Frances Cabrini *Church*. The *Church* believes in the sanctity of life. The phrase "separation of *church* and state" is nowhere in the Constitution.
Cite (v) Site (n) Sight (n)	*Cite* (v)—list a source of information, to quote *Site* (n)—a place *Sight* (n)—vision, as in eye sight	Integrity demands you *cite* your sources properly. The *site* the original pilgrims used for their first community was called Plymouth Plantation. Benjamin Franklin's *sight* was so bad, he invented bifocals for himself.

Cleanup (adj, n) Clean up (v)	*Cleanup* (adj)—a cleaning *Cleanup* (n)—backup, reserve, fourth hitter on a baseball team *Clean* up (v)—to clean	Many say the world's best *cleanup* hitter in baseball is Colorado Rockies Troy Tulowitzki. Virtually all of government needs a *cleanup.* How many times have your parents said, "*Clean up* your room"?
Close proximity (adj)	Omit *proximity.*	The Capitol building is *close* to the White House, about seven minutes by car.
Coarse (adj) Course (n)	*Coarse* (adj)—rough in texture *Course* (n)—a route followed *Course* (n)—a dish as part of a meal	Rubbing *coarse* sandpaper over wood makes the wood smooth. The Declaration of Independence: "When in the *Course* of human events, it becomes necessary for one people to dissolve the political bands which have connected them with another…" The pilgrims' dessert, usually the last *course* in a meal, included a prune tart seasoned with rosemary, rosewater, and cinnamon, and sweetened with sugar.
Colons (p) Semicolons (p)	Colons—used to introduce a thought or list Semicolons—used to join two, related sentences.	The Founders brought forth twenty-seven grievances to King George III; the first one was imposing taxes on the people without their permission. The Declaration of Independence was not completely signed on July 4, 1776; most of the signatories did so on August 2.
College University	While they both mean higher education, English speakers outside the USA often use the generic *university* (not requiring a modifier like *the*). In America, we use *college.*	Due to its high cost, low return on investment, and leftist indoctrination, more people should avoid going to *college* immediately after high school, especially if they are unsure of their major.

AMERICA THE GRAMMAR

Commas (p)	For two items, no comma. Use *and, but,* or *or.*	Between liberty *and* tyranny, which will you fight for?
	For three or more items, use a comma after each item except the last. This is called the Oxford comma.	4th Amendment: The right of the people to be secure in their *persons, houses, papers, and effects*, against unreasonable searches and seizures, shall not be violated…"
	Note on commas. As a rule, place a comma before conjunctions (and, but, or, for, so, yet) if it is followed by an independent clause. Mostly, *quit using so many*. If you say the sentence out loud, generally speaking, put a comma where you take a breath.	
Compare (v) Contrast (v)	*Compare* (v)—to find similarities *Contrast* (n)—state of being different *Contrast* (v)—to find differences	Never *compare* yourself to others; you could become vain or bitter. It is easy to *contrast* the values of America with those of, for example, Iran, whose people are not free to pursue their own happiness. We should be able to articulate the *contrast* between individual racism and systemic racism.
Compare to Compare with	Generally, these are the same. If you get a nitpicking English teacher, however, I agree with Strunk and White: when comparing two objects thought to be different and you wish to point out their similarities, use *to*. Use *with* when comparing objects thought to be similar and you wish to point out their differences.	The United States *compares* to Mexico in that the predominant religion is Christianity. American exceptionalism is not a statement of pride but a statistical fact. When you *compare* the founding principles of all countries *with* those of the United States, no country started with the notion of God-given, inalienable rights of life, liberty, and the pursuit of happiness.

Complement (n) Compliment (n, v)	*Complement* (n)—something that goes well with or completes another. *Compliment* (n)—praise or flattery. *Compliment* (v)—to praise	Jelly *complements* peanut butter. The best reply to any *compliment* is a simple "Thank you." We should *compliment* people when they do good things for others in need.
Comprise (v)	*Comprise* (v)—to contain or include. However, some sources say the word means both contain and make up. When in doubt, use *compose* or *make up*	The first ten Amendments *comprise* the Bill of Rights.
Conscience (n) Conscious (adj) Consciousness (n)	*Conscience* (n)—inner feeling of right and wrong *Conscious* (adj)—awake or aware, deliberate Conscious (n)—part of the brain containing psychic material *Consciousness* (n)—state of being conscious	To have a *conscience*, a mental "alarm" goes off in us when we don't behave properly. From the Bible: Mark 5:30 says, "And straight away Jesus was *conscious* that power had gone out of him." Each time legislators make *conscious* decisions to ignore the Constitution, our freedoms fade. We must regain our *consciousness* about American values.
Copyright (n, adj) Copywriter (n)	*Copyright* (n)—legal right to creative works, commonly in writing and music. *Copyright* (adj)—referring to the copyright law *Copywriter* (n)—one who produces copy for published works including brochures, texts, books, etc.	The *copyright* on the book you are reading now means you cannot reproduce what I have written without permission. Ironically, the world would be better if despotic countries would violate the *copyright* on the Declaration of Independence. The *copywriter* plagiarized his work and was soon fired.
Core (adj, n) Corps (n) Corpse (n)	*Core* (n)—center of an object *Corps* (n, pronounced "core")—an organization *Corpse* (n)—a dead, human body	Global warming alarmists claim the earth's *core* temperature is rising. The Marine *Corps*, which began in 1775, has produced many *corpses* that were formerly bad people.

AMERICA THE GRAMMAR

Could of Should of Would of	Proper usage: *could have, should have, would have*	If I *could have* and *should have*, I *would have*.
Council (n) Counsel (n, v) Consul (v)	*Council* (n)—legislative or rule-making body *Counsel* (n)—legal adviser *Counsel* (v)—to confer with or seek advice *Consul* (n)—government official	The *Council* on Foreign Relations provides up-to-date information and analysis about world events and American foreign policy. The Sixth Amendment: in all criminal prosecutions, the accused shall enjoy the right to a speedy and public trial… and to have the assistance of *counsel* for his defense. Husbands and wives should *counsel* with each other before making big spending decisions. A *consul* is different from an ambassador in that he deals in matters of individuals versus those of state officials.
Couple (n) Couple of	*Couple of* (n)—expression to indicate two items. Sources go back and forth on the proper usage, so use your judgment.	There are more than a *couple* states that allow for constitutional carry, which means no permit is required to carry a concealed firearm.
Criteria (n) Criterion	*Criterion* (n)—single standard by which a decision is made *Criteria* (n)—plural of criterion	One of the many *criteria* used to determine whom you should marry includes a belief in God. Another *criterion* should be whether you enjoy the same pizza. Don't laugh; it's important.
Cue (n, v) Queue (n, v)	*Cue* (n)—a sign/signal that prompts action *Cue* (v)—to give a sign/signal *Queue* (n)—a line of people or things *Queue* (v)—to line up or wait in a line	When acting in a play, always be ready for your *cue*. The stage manager *cued* me to start my lines during the play. In communist countries, the *queues* of people waiting for bread are long. *Queue* the concert fans so they can get tickets.

Dash (p)	Longer than a hyphen, a dash separates words or clauses or indicates an abrupt halt to speech. Commas can be swapped for dashes to make your writing stand out a bit more. Don't overuse them. See also "Punctuation Marks" section.	For their work in codifying the emancipation of black slaves, the following are often called the Civil War Amendments—the 13th, 14th, and 15th Amendments. "There is no perfect woma—"—the minute before I met my wife.
Definite (adj) Definate	*Definite* (adj)—distinct, assured, not vague *Definate* is incorrect	Conservatives do not lack *definite* purpose but rather the courage to do what is necessary to promote the cause of freedom.
Desert (n, v) Dessert (n)	*Desert* (n)—dry, arid place often made of sand *Desert* (v)—abandon *Dessert* (n)—generally the last course of a meal, usually sweet	One of the greatest feats of American ingenuity is our ability to live in the middle of *deserts*. No worthy member of the military would ever *desert* his unit or a fallen man. *Desserts* eaten during the Civil War included hardtack, a type of biscuit made from flour, water, and salt.
Disassemble (v) Dissemble (v)	*Dissemble* (v)—fake or pretend *Disassemble* (v)—opposite of assemble, to take apart	Do not *dissemble* liking a friend because her parents are wealthy. A valuable skill is to be able to *disassemble* a car and put it back together.
Do's (n) Don'ts (n)	If you do not use an apostrophe with "do," it will look like the Spanish word for two (dos).	The first ten Amendments, often called the Bill of Rights, is a list of government *don'ts* versus government *do's*.
Double negatives	Double negatives equal positives so if you say *We don't have no*, you are admitting you have some.	We *don't* have *any* excuse for not protecting our southern border.
Doubtful (adj) Doubtless (adj)	*Doubtful*—having doubt *Doubtless*—having no doubt	It's *doubtful* the United States would have been created without the Boston Massacre or the Boston Tea Party.

AMERICA THE GRAMMAR

Dived/Dove (v)	*Dove* (v)—past tense of to dive. *Dived* appears to be an old usage.	Our Founding Fathers <u>*dove*</u> into politics even though many of them had never held office.
Drank (v) Drunk (v, adj)	*Drank* (v)—past tense of drink *Drunk* (v)—past participle of drink *Drunk* (adj)—inebriated, intoxicated	During Prohibition, you did not commit a crime if you <u>*drank*</u> alcohol; the punishment was only if you manufactured, distributed, and sold it. While trying to surf ocean waves, many times I have <u>*drunk*</u> saltwater. Even local school board members have been <u>*drunk*</u> on power.
Drier (adj) Dryer (n)	*Drier* (adj)—more dry. *Dryer* (n)—machine that dries	Clothes are <u>*drier*</u> when left in the <u>*dryer*</u> longer.
Due to the fact that	Use *since* or *because*	<u>*Since*</u> the Federalist Papers were written by people using the pseudonym Publius, we cannot be certain who wrote each paper.
E.g. or i.e.	e.g.—Latin *exempli gratia* (for example) i.e.—Latin *id est* (in other words)	There are many things about Thomas Jefferson people do not know (<u>*e.g.*</u>, He taught his twelve grandchildren to play a board game called Goose.) The United States already has two forms of socialized medicine (<u>*i.e.*</u>, Medicare and Medicaid).
Elicit (v) Illicit (adj)	*Elicit* (v)—to evoke or draw out *Illicit* (adj)—illegal	The Star-Spangled Banner <u>*elicits*</u> chills and a lump in my throat. The use of <u>*illicit*</u> drugs is virtually guaranteed to hurt your chances for a good life.
Ellipses	See also "Punctuation Marks" section.	Three (3) dots only Did you know states can change the constitution any time they want? Article V tells us how: …the Legislatures of two thirds of the…States, shall call a Convention for proposing Amendments, which,…shall be valid to all Intents and Purposes, as Part of this Constitution…

Etc. (adv)	Latin for *et cetera*. This error mostly has to do with pronunciation. Too many mistakenly people pronounce it "ECK-set-er-ah." The other rule concerns when you use it in a series. Generally, use etc. as the third in a series of items.	"That among these are life, liberty, *etc*." Do not forget that last part.
either/or (adv) neither/nor (adv)	Comparing two parts of sentence, noun or verb	He wanted *either* to run *or* hide against the attackers; honor and duty made him fight. He wanted *neither* the Camaro *nor* Mustang, knowing. the Corvette was faster.
Emigrate (v) Immigrate (v)	*Emigrate* (v)—to leave the country you are in for permanent residence *Immigrate* (v)—to enter a country you are not not a native of for permanent residence	If the United States falls, where can we *emigrate* to that provides the same freedoms? Americans should not blame people who *immigrate* to the United States, but immigrants should work hard to become part of the American culture.
Eminent (adj) Imminent (adj)	*Eminent* (adj)—prominent, well-known *Imminent* (adj)—impending, immediate	Two, *eminent* economists worth reading are Thomas Sowell and Walter E. Williams. We cannot prevent all *imminent* danger; all we can do is prepare for worst-case scenarios.
Empathy (n) Sympathy (n)	*Empathy* (n)—understanding the situation or condition of another. The key word is understanding without actually having gone through the same experience. *Sympathy* (n)—feeling the emotions of what another is going through, such as the death of a loved one.	Every time I see a member of the military say goodbye to his family when he leaves them, I have *empathy* for how sad his family feels. Those who have successfully built their own businesses have *sympathy* for those struggling to build their own.

AMERICA THE GRAMMAR

Endemic (adj) Epidemic (n) Pandemic (n)	*Endemic* (adj)—limited to a particular area, region, or group of people *Epidemic* (n)—a disease affecting a large number of people in a given area or group (larger than endemic) *Pandemic* (n)—a disease outbreak affecting the country, continent, or earth (larger than epidemic)	Chickenpox is *endemic* since it usually affects only young children. The *epidemic* across the city caused government officials to overstep their authority. Malaria is a *pandemic* in Africa that could be prevented if the pesticide DDT was allowed to be used against mosquitos.
Envious (adj) Jealous (adj)	*Envious* (adj)—feeling of wanting the same as someone else *Jealous* (adj)—fear of losing what you have to someone else	If you are *envious* of what someone else has, work hard to earn it for yourself. Being *jealous* in relationships will almost certainly cause you and your significant other pain.
Everyday (adj) Every day (n)	*Everyday* (adj)—commonplace, typical *Every day* (n)—each day	The free market is responsible for technological advancements on *everyday* things like thermostats you can control from anywhere. Those who pray *every day* tend to be more grateful for what they have.
Everybody (n) Every body (n) Everyone (n) Every one (n)	*Everybody* (pronoun)—every person *Every body* (n)—each, physical body *Everyone* (n), *Every one* (n)—each one Both words mean the same, but using *body* with *every* is less formal.	According to the Sixth Amendment, *everyone* in the United States has the right to a trial by jury. What happened to *every one* of the cast members of the original *Star Wars*?
Exact same (adv)	*Exact* (adj)—not approximate, precise. Since it is an adverb, use *exact* sparingly.	There are twenty-six remaining copies of the Declaration of Independence, each *the same* as the other.
Fair (adj, n) Fare (n)	*Fair* (adj)—equitable or acceptable *Fair* (n)—exhibition *Fare* (n)—a fee for service *Fare* (n)—food or drink	Many people are in favor of a *Fair Tax*, which eliminates all income tax and pose a 23 percent tax on all sales.

		The Minnesota State *Fair* is the largest state fair in the nation and home to great *fare* including the best cheese curds on the planet.
		It is typical to pay drivers a ~15 percent tip in addition to the *fare*.
Famous (adj) Infamous (adj) Notorious (adj)	*Famous* (adj)—well-known, popular, generally in a positive way	Our Founding Fathers were considered *famous* by the colonists but *notorious* by King George III.
	Infamous and *notorious* (adj)—well known or popular, generally in a negative way	
Farther (adv) Further (adv, v)	*Farther* (adv)—refers to physical distance	When jogging, always go *farther* than you think you can.
	Further (adv)—refers to an advance of degree	The *further* along state legislatures get in approving Article 5 Convention of States, the closer we are to reigning in government overreach.
	Further (v)—advance a position or cause, promote	You will *further* your career if you keep learning more about the industry you are in.
Faze (v) Phase (n, v)	*Faze* (v)—to disturb	Against formidable odds, if General George Washington was ever *fazed*, he never showed it.
	Phase (n)—stage in a project	
	Phase (v)—carry out or execute in parts	The Articles of Confederation could be considered a *phase* of the Constitution, as the former led to the Constitution we use today.
		Going from never working out to immediately running an ultramarathon is not recommended; you should *phase* in longer workouts over time.
Fearful, Fearsome	*Fearful* (adj)—to be frightened	Far too many governments are *fearsome*; they all need to be *fearful* of the people they mean to serve.
	Fearsome (adj)—worthy of being frightened by others	

AMERICA THE GRAMMAR

Faint (adj, v) Feint (n, v)	*Faint* (adj)—lacking brightness, vividness, clearness, loudness, and strength *Faint* (v)—to lose consciousness *Feint* (n)—a fake move or attack *Feint* (v)—to fake an attack or other action	The colors of the US flag should never be *faint*. When a person *faints*, his blood vessels open too wide or the heartbeat slows, causing a lack of blood flow to the brain. A *feint* is a good move in boxing or martial arts as it distracts your opponent from receiving the real strike. The UFC champion *feinted* a right jab and finished his opponent with a left cross.
Fiancé (n) Fiancée (n)	*Fiancé* (n)—man who's planning on getting married *Fiancée* (n)—woman who's planning on getting married	Gentlemen, as a *fiancé*, one of the greatest gifts you can give your *fiancée* is premarital counseling.
For all intents and purposes, sometimes confused with for all *intensive* purposes	Use *essentially* or *basically* instead.	If the United States runs out of money and China and other countries quit lending to us, we are *basically* done as a country.
For free, Free	If you offer something without charging for it, leave out the *for*.	Learn this rule, and commit it to memory: nothing is *free*.
Going to, Gonna	*Gonna* is incorrect.	To aid in your learning, I am *going to* repeat the previously stated rule: nothing is free.
God, god	Use *God* when referring to the name of God and *god* when referring to the generic and nontheological God.	Dear *God*, please bless the United States of America. Anyone who behaves as if he is a *god* will soon enough learn the truth. There is one, and it isn't He.
Gone (v) Went (v)	*Gone* (v)—past participle of go and requires words like has, have, had, is, am, are, was, were, and be. *Went* (v)—used as a past tense and doesn't require these words.	Many times, I *have gone* to the gym to work out, wishing I could be elsewhere but afterward was glad I *went*.

Good (adj, n) Well (adv)	We have arrived at one of the golden errors. Remember that *good* is an adjective and *well* is an adverb, and you will know what to use.	Ephesians 2:10: "For we are God's handiwork, created in Christ Jesus to do *good* works, which God prepared in advance for us to do." The Salvation Army does *good*. In greetings, when asked, "How are you doing?" the response is *well*. But if you are asked, "How are you?" the response is *good*, as it describes you the noun. She is a *good* soccer player because she often does *well*.
Got (v) Gotten (v)	*Got* (v)—past participle of get. Generally, *got* and *gotten* are used in informal speech and writing. They both sound bad and are unnecessary. Use them sparingly.	You should *get* what you earn. Yesterday, I *got* a black eye for smarting off to my mother. Many times, I *have gotten* a speeding ticket because I was driving angry.
Gray (adj) Grey (adj)	*Gray* (adj)—American usage of the color. Tip: "a" for American *Grey* (adj)—non-American usage of the color	Do not be afraid to marry the one you love. There is great peace and adventure in growing old and *gray* with each other.
Grisly (adj) Grizzly (n)	*Grisly* (adj)—gory, disgusting *Grizzly* (n)—a brown bear	One of the most *grisly* Civil War battles was the Battle of Antietam that took more than twenty-three thousand soldiers' lives over twelve hours. Whenever I would challenge my dad, he would always say, "You would rather bite a *grizzly* in the butt."
Hanged (v) Hung (adj)	*Hanged* (v)—capital punishment of a human being *Hung* (adj)—refers to objects that are put up on walls	The last criminal *hanged* in the United States was Billy Bailey in 1996. I *hung* a copy of the Declaration of Independence above my office desk.
Heal (v) Heel (n)	*Heal* (n)—make healthy or better *Heel* (v)—back portion of a foot, end portion of a loaf of bread	After the Civil War where brother fought brother, our country needed to *heal*.

AMERICA THE GRAMMAR

		The term Achilles *heel* came from the Greek warrior Achilles, who was dipped by his mother in the River Styx by his ankles. Since his ankles did not receive the magical waters of the River, his *heels* were vulnerable.
Hear (v) Here (n)	*Hear* (v)—receive sound through your ear. To help you remember what to use, hear has ear.	Whenever you *hear* the National Anthem, take off your hat, and put your right hand over your heart.
	Here (n)—a specific place	*Here*, in this country, we have everything we need to accomplish our goals.
Heroine (n) Heroin (n)	*Heroin* (n)—opium-derived narcotic	Look up what *heroin* does to the human mind and body, and you will see why it is one of the most potent poisons on earth.
	Heroine (n)—female character in a story	One of the greatest American *heroines* is Emily Geiger, who, during the Revolutionary War, swallowed a secret message intended to seek reinforcements against the British.
Hippie (n) Hippy (adj)	*Hippie* (n)—person often associated by dress or attitude as having been influenced by or resembles the 1960s peace movement	Never, under any circumstance, tell a pregnant woman she has become *hippy*, not even if she truly is a *hippie*.
	Hippy (adj)—having large hips	
Hyphen (p)	Hyphens, shorter than dashes, join words or clauses.	Catastrophic, *man-made* global warming is hard to act on because we must prove all three together: the earth is warming, man is the cause, and it is catastrophic.
	Hyphens are only used to modify words if they appear before the word, not after.	
	See also "Punctuation Marks" section.	For example, if global warming is not *man made* but a natural occurrence, there is nothing we can do about it.
If (prep) Whether (conj)	*If* (prep)—used to express a condition.	*If* the American people are free to live as they wish, please explain to me the problem in this.
	Whether (conj)—used to express alternatives.	

	If you really want to improve your speaking and writing, leave out *not* when using *whether*.	*Whether* it's a soft tyranny or hard tyranny, why would you settle for either?
Impactful (adj)	For a few reasons, *impactful* is an incorrect conflation of *impact* (n, v, adj) and *influential* (adj). Use *influential*.	The Law of the Sea Treaty is an *influential* agreement that will affect how our ships can navigate in every ocean.
Imply (v) Infer (v)	*Imply* (v)—convey a message without explicitly saying the words *Infer* (v)—How or whether you, the receiver, interpret a message	When a legislator *implies* that she's willing to vote on a bill before she reads it, there's little hope we can have that she will take her work seriously. When President George W. Bush said, "My fellow Americans, let's roll." I *inferred* that he meant to deal with the perpetrators of the attacks of 9/11.
In regards to (phrase) Regarding (prep)	Remember one of the golden rules of communication: If you can say something in few words, do it. *In regard to* (no "s" on regard) is fine, but it's long. Use *regarding* instead.	*Regarding* how a man whose past we know little about could achieve the Office of the President of the United States is a mystery to me.
In spite of (phrase) Despite (prep)	Same rule as *regarding*. *In spite of* and *despite* mean the same, so for good writing, use *despite*.	*Despite* spending thousands of dollars—sometimes hundreds of thousands—on a bachelor's degree, more people are discovering how wasteful colleges are.
Incent (v) Incentivize (v)	I used to argue against *incent* as a verb because until recently, it wasn't a word, a mix up of incite or encourage. Many words make themselves into our vocabulary, and this one seems to have merit at least in a business sense. *Incent* (v)—to encourage with remuneration such as money or gifts. *Incentivize* (v) is a bit ugly, so avoid if you can.	Let's *incent* savings by only taxing what we spend. This is called the Fair Tax.
Incredible (adj) Incredulous (adj)	*Incredible* (adj)—hard to believe, usually in a good way *Incredulous* (adj)—describing how you doubt something is true	Knowing what could have and did become of many of our Founders' families and estates for challenging the King George III, the courage of our Founders was *incredible*.

AMERICA THE GRAMMAR

		When I tell them the constitution can be changed by states invoking Article V, it is understandable that people are *incredulous*.
In order to (conj)	Omit *in order*, and only use *to*.	I'll give the writers of the Declaration of Independence some leeway by not using *To* when they wrote in the Preeamble "*In order to* form a more perfect union..."
Irregardless	Because of "less," the *irr* makes this redundant and incorrect. Use *regardless* or *irrespective*.	*Regardless* of what happens during your lifetime, you always have a choice as to how you react.
Itch (n, v) Scratch (v)	*Itch* (n)—uncomfortable sensation	*Scratch* that *itch*.
	Itch (v)—to cause an itch	
	Scratch (v)—to cut or damage with a rough item, to rub part of your body with a rough item	
It's Its	It's = It is	*It's* of utmost importance to be involved in politics; surely, *it is* involved in you.
	Its = possessive of *it*	You are responsible for your country; *its* care is up to you.
Jewelry (n)	Incorrect to spell it *jewelery*	One of the biggest *jewelry* heists was worth approximately $136 million.
Judgment (n)	Incorrect to spell it *judgement*	Pascal's Wager goes something like this: I would rather live my life believing there is a God and come to find there isn't, than live my life believing there isn't a God and, come *judgment* day, find out that there is.
Lay (v) Lie (v) Lain (v)	To recline or lower	Today, I *lie* down. Yesterday, I *lay* down.
	Lie (v)—present tense	Many times, I have *lain* down.
	Lay (v)—past tense	When it applies to an object
	Lain (v)—past participle	Israeli Knesset Chairman Benjamin Netanyahu: "if the Arabs *lay* down their arms there will be no more war, but if Israel *lays* down its weapons there would be no more Israel."
		Yesterday, I *laid* my book down to listen to my teacher.
		Many times, I have *laid* my bike down without using the kickstand.

29

Lend (v) Loan (n)	*Lend, Loan* (v)—opposite of borrow, when you give something with intention of being paid back. *Lend* (v)—can also mean to impart or contribute *Loan* (n)—the thing borrowed	Do not <u>*loan*</u> your money to anyone who has a passport in his hands and an airport shuttle waiting; those two factors <u>*lend*</u> themselves to the possibility of never seeing your money again. If you receive a <u>*loan*</u>, you are obligated to pay it back.
Less (adj), Fewer (adj)	*Less* (adj)—things you cannot count *Fewer* (adj)—things you can count	There is definitely <u>*less*</u> stress when there are <u>*fewer*</u> children in your home, but there is the potential for more joy.
Lets (v), Let's	*Lets* (v)—third-person singular form of the verb let. *Let's* (v)—Let us	Great is the successful man who <u>*lets*</u> others believe they did it themselves. <u>*Let's*</u> begin to take back our country.
Liable (adj), Libel (n)	*Liable* (adj)—legally responsible *Libel* (n)—legal tort in the written word. Slander is the legal tort in the spoken word	Every American is <u>*liable*</u> for the continuation of the United States and our way of life. If you write something online or in a newspaper that is false against another person or organization, you could be sued for <u>*libel*</u>.
Like (adv)	*Like* (adv) isn't bad; it's just unnecessary and used far too often as a filler word.	I drank <u>*like*</u> four Red Bulls that night, <u>*like*</u>, right before bed. I didn't <u>*like*</u> sleep for a few days. If the above is hard to read, please understand how it is to hear.
Literally (adv)	As with like, *literally* (adv) is an incorrectly used or overused word. If you take a moment to think about what you're saying, you will find it should rarely be used.	My head <u>*literally*</u> exploded. Really? If that were the case, you wouldn't be able to say, "My head <u>*literally*</u> exploded."
Long story short	An expression used to indicate you are about to conclude your story. If you say this, you're making the story longer, so just say the short part of your story or begin the phrase with "So" or "In short."	So don't eat Tide Pods.
Loose (adj), Lose (v)	*Loose* (adj)—opposite of tight *Lose* (v)—to misplace, to find yourself without, to not win	Set the hounds <u>*loose*</u>. Once you <u>*lose*</u> your freedom, you rarely get it back.

AMERICA THE GRAMMAR

Majority are, Majority is	What determines which you use is the object of the preposition (*majority of X*). With things you can count, use *majority are*. With things you cannot count, use *majority is*.	The *majority* of the Amendments *are* for protecting Americans' rights. A simple *majority is* sufficient to pass many laws.
May (v), Might (v)	*May* (v)—expresses a possibility and is more likely than might. It also asks for permission ("May I?" versus "Can I?"). *Might* (v)—less likely than may	*May* I get up from my desk? When I told my teacher I *might* skip school tomorrow, she said we *may* have a test.
Maybe (adv), May be (phrase)	*Maybe* (adv)—perhaps *May be* (v phrase)—could be	*Maybe* we should stay on the road. We *may be* in for hard times if we don't learn self-reliance.
Medal (n), Meddle (v), Metal (n), Mettle (n)	*Medal* (n)—item won during a competition *Meddle* (v)—to interfere in the affairs of another *Metal* (n)—substance usually mined *Mettle* (n)—gumption, character	Michael Phelps has the record of most gold *medals* at twenty-three. Unless they ask, and preferably not even then, don't *meddle* in the relationship of a guy and his girlfriend. At room temperature, all of the *metals* on the Periodic Table of Elements are solids except for mercury, a liquid. Though Eddie the Eagle, the ski jumper, finished dead last in the Winter Olympics, experts agree he had *mettle*.
Method (n), Methodology (n)	*Method* (n)—procedure for accomplishing a task or goal. *Methodology* (n)—study of methods	His *methods* are unorthodox, but Robin Williams' character in *Dead Poets Society* made him a great teacher. The easiest way to succeed in life is to study the *methodologies* of people who are successful, and do what they do.
Myriad (n, adj)	*Myriad* (n)—a multitude *Myriad* (adj)—numerous, countless	There are *a myriad* of reasons to love America. There are *myriad* reasons to love America.

	The traditional definition used to be that *myriad* was not a noun, so many people were using the word incorrectly. However, when many people use a word incorrectly, it often becomes acceptable. You'll avoid a hassle if you quit using it.	
Nauseated (n), Nauseous (n)	*Nauseated* (adj)—traditional definition of means you feel like vomiting. *Nauseous* (adj)—something or someone makes you want to vomit. The two are used interchangeably such that even Merriam-Webster makes no distinction.	When a public servant abuses her office, it makes me *nauseated/nauseous*.
Needs [x] (v)	*Needs ironed* is incorrect. *Ironed* in this case is an adjective, so the sentence is nonsensical.	All clothes *need to be washed* (not *need washed*) eventually.
Nip it in the butt	Nip it in the *bud* is correct.	His habit of sleeping in until noon needs to be *nipped in the bud*.
Noone (pro)	*No one* is correct	*No one* is free from the obligation of choosing to be happy.
Nuclear (adj)	Pronounced *New-CLEE-er*	Everyone claiming to be an environmentalist should support *nuclear* energy.
Numbering one through 10	This depends on what style guide you are using. According to the AP Style, you spell out the word until the number 10. Always write out the word of a number when it begins a sentence.	One, two, three, four, five, six, seven, eight, nine, 10, 11, 12… *Four* horsemen occupy part of the book of Revelations.
Numbers with apostrophes	Don't use apostrophes to make a word plural. However, apostrophes should be used when it would confuse the reader otherwise.	The pilgrims first landed in what is now the United States in the early 1600s. My teacher was supposed to use uppercase letters for grades on my assignment but instead gave me three "a's."
Nuptial (adj, n)	*Nuptial* (adj)—another name for or related to wedding. Sometimes misspelled as *Nuptual*.	The *nuptial* blessing in Catholic weddings is often conducted after the exchange of vows.

AMERICA THE GRAMMAR

OK, okay	Okay is more formal. Naturally, on social media, "OK" is acceptable.	According 4 US Code Ch. 1, as long as the US Flag is not on the ground, it is _okay_ to leave it out in the rain.
Old fashion, Old-fashioned	If you're speaking of outdated or outmoded beliefs or style, _old-fashioned_ is correct.	If I had a dancing style, you would definitely call it _old-fashioned_.
Optimal (adj) Optimum (n, adj)	Both mean _favorable_.	Generally speaking, the _optimal_ use of government is when a given department acts like a sheriff and only gets involved when something goes wrong.
Orient, Orientate	_Orient_ (v)—to align or position, adjust _Orientate_ (v)—to align or position, adjust The British tend to use _orientate_ and Americans uses _orient_	For safety, always _orient_ yourself with the exits when out in public.
Over-exaggerated (adj)	_Exaggerated_ (adj)—overstated, embellished. "Over" is unnecessary.	One of the more _exaggerated_ facts about the Second Amendment is that it was written to give citizens the ability to hunt animals. Instead, it was largely for defense against a tyrannical government.
Overlook (v), Oversee (v)	Overlook—to forget or pass over, is usually a bad thing Oversee—usually a good thing if done correctly, is to manage or supervise someone or something	She _overlooked_ the fact that the Constitution does not actually call for nationalized health care. While governors _oversee_ how states spend their budgets, many rely on the state legislature to provide a budget bill to guide them.
Palate (n), Palette (n), Pallet (n)	_Palate_ (n)—roof of the mouth _Palette_ (n)—a flat board a painter uses to mix paints _Pallet_ (n)—wooden platform used for shipping	Many people require _palate_ expanders to help straighten their teeth. Using his color _palette_, the legendary Bob Ross, a famous painter on PBS, always made painting seem easy. Moving fifty-pound bags of cement from a _pallet_ is great exercise.
Parameter (n), Perimeter (n)	_Parameter_ (n)—a limitation regarding how a task can be accomplished	The _parameters_ of all governing laws are that they are created by man, and that means they will never be perfect.

	Perimeter (n)—a boundary restricting a certain area	School campuses usually have definite *perimeter* lines to keep young kids from going out and strangers from coming in.
Parentheses (p)	See also "Punctuation Marks" section.	In general, parentheses should be used to add clarity to a sentence that wouldn't be clear without them.
Paramount (adj), Tantamount (adj)	*Paramount* (adj)—crucial, most important *Tantamount* (adj)—equivalent	It's *paramount* that you learn essential math; name one thing you use daily that doesn't require it. A pitcher of Coke is *tantamount* to a six pack.
Participial phrases	Words containing a participle (verb +-ing or -ed, -en, -d, -t, -n, or -ne), a modifier, and a pronoun or noun phrase. Errors occur when the action doesn't make sense with the noun. Error Example: Signing the Declaration of Independence, the document became a symbol of freedom. In this sentence, the participial phrase "Signing the Declaration of Independence" suggests that the document itself was performing the action of signing.	A better way to say this could be "After signing the Declaration of Independence, the founding fathers turned a simple and formerly blank piece of parchment into a rare symbol of freedom."
Patience (n), Patients (n)	*Patience* (n)—tolerance *Patients* (n)—plural of patient, as in medical patient	*Patience* is one of the greatest gifts you can give yourself and your family. A free-market medical system puts the power of choice in the hands of *patients* versus hospitals or corporations.
Prerogative (n)	*Prerogative* (n)—often misspelled as perogative, a right or privilege usually for a group or class of people	Owning our freedom is the *prerogative* of every American.
Personal (adj) Personnel (n)	*Personal* (adj)—regarding one's particular life, relationships, and emotions *Personnel* (adj)—a group of people, as in those employed by a company	Why is it when someone says, "It's nothing *personal*," it almost always feels like it is? We should honor all military *personnel* for their service.

AMERICA THE GRAMMAR

Perspective (n), Prospective (n)	*Perspective* (n)—a particular point of view *Prospective* (n)—potential or likely	The *perspective* of the Founding Fathers was "We've had enough of your bad rule, King George. We're starting our own country." This position laid the groundwork for *prospective* changes that would make the United States what it is today.
Persuade (v), Convince (v)	*Persuade* (v)—influence an action *Convince* (v)—change a thought	Despite the bitter cold and far too many soldiers without coats and shoes, General George Washington *persuaded* his officers and enlisted men to cross the Delaware River that night to win the Battle of Trenton. You will never *convince* me that there isn't a God.
Peruse (v)	*Peruse* (v)—often misunderstood to mean to review or look over in a cursory or haphazard manner, actually means to look through carefully	To speak intelligently on it, each of us should *peruse* the Constitution.
Perverse (adj), Perverted (adj)	*Perverse* (adj)—awkward or opposite *Perverted* (adj)—twisted or corrupt	It may seem *perverse* that too many untalented people get to be on *American Idol*, but it is by far the funniest part of the show. Too many have a *perverted* interpretation of the Koran.
Phenomena (n), Phenomenon (n)	*Phenomenon* (n)—singular of a particular situation that is difficult to explain *Phenomena* (n)—plural of phenomenon.	With his one-inch punch, Bruce Lee was a *phenomenon*. The *phenomena* of Parkour is fun to watch.
Pickup (n), Pick up (phrase)	*Pickup* (n)—a truck *Pick up* (v)—to grab something, often from the floor or ground	We used to ride in the back of the *pickup*. If you had a dime for the number of times your mother told you to *pick up* your room, you could pay someone to pick it up for you.
Poisonous (adj), Venomous (adj)	*Poisonous* (adj)—transfer of toxin from touch or ingestion (eating) *Venomous* (adj)—transfer of venom via sting, bite, or spit	In the United States, there is only one *poisonous* frog but twenty *venomous* snakes.

Pom-pom (n), Pompom (n), Pompon (n)	All spellings acceptable, pompoms are regarded as the frilly things cheerleaders shake to stir up a crowd but have been used in various sizes and shapes on soldiers' uniforms.	A new movie is coming out about a cheerleader whose <u>*pompoms*</u> are made of razor wire.
Possessives	One of the best books on grammar, usage, and style is *The Elements of Style* by William Strunk and E. B. White. To make a noun possessive, they say to add "'s" to the end of any word. Wrong. Two examples: Achilles's Heel Jesus's teachings It's too complicated. Use *'s* if the word doesn't end in *s*, and just add an apostrophe when it does.	John's books Jesus' teachings Achilles' Heel The Jones' Christmas card
Possessives (Multiple)	I've honestly heard people say, "John and I's book." The easiest way to remember the rule is to consider what you would use if you removed one of the two names or pronoun: "John's book" "My book" A book that belongs to both John and me. *John's and my book.* When we're talking about John's truck and my Lamborghini, use *John's and my cars.*	
Predominant (adj), Predominate (v)	*Predominant* (adj)—the strongest, most popular, or most powerful *Predominate* (v)—to influence or control by large number, status, or power	Conservatism, a <u>*predominant*</u> political philosophy, is more accurately described as a science of observation of what works for society and what doesn't. Muslims <u>*predominate*</u> in the Middle East.

AMERICA THE GRAMMAR

Premier (adj), Premiere (n)	*Premier* (adj)—first, inaugural *Premiere* (n)—first public appearance or showing	The *premier* iPhone changed the mobile computing world. Abraham Lincoln was assassinated at the *premiere* of the play *Our American Cousin*.
Prescribe (v), Proscribe (v)	*Prescribe* (v)—advise or authorize use of medical treatment *Proscribe* (v)—forbid or ban. Not used often	He asked his doctor to *prescribe* antibiotics after being stuck for several hours on an airplane. Burning the US flag is not *proscribed* by law, but it's disrespectful to all Americans, especially those who served in the military.
Pronouns: I, Me, He/Him, She/Her, We/Us, They/Them (pro), Myself/Himself/Herself/Ourselves/Themselves	The misuse of pronouns is one of the most common mistakes in American linguistic history, particularly *I*/*me*. The origin goes back a long time and is mostly a result of Catholic nuns, twelve-inch rulers, and sore knuckles. For the record, *me* is not always wrong, and the attempt to force *I* where it does not belong makes the situation worse. There are pronouns that are subjects in a sentence (that perform the action) and pronouns that are objects in a sentence (that receive the action). When the pronoun is a <u>subject</u> of the sentence, use *I, he, she, we, they,* or *it*. When the pronoun is the <u>object</u> of the sentence, use *me, him, her, us, them,* or *it*.	<u>Subject</u> I sit in class. He sits in class. She sits in class. She and I sit in class. We sit in class. They sit in class. <u>Object</u> The teacher gave me an A. The teacher gave him an A. The teacher gave her an A. The teacher gave us an A. The teacher gave them an A. The teacher gave it another try. <u>Object with multiple pronoun</u> The teacher gave him and me an A. The teach gave her and him an A. The teacher gave them and us an A. Copy *me* (not myself) on that email. To dislodge the food stuck in his throat, he gave *himself* the Heimlich maneuver by forcefully bending over the chair. She smacked *herself* on the head when she realized how silly she sounded.

People get messed up when we encounter multiple pronouns (he and I, her and me, etc.). When you see more than one pronoun and don't know if you should use subjective or objective pronouns, use this trick: *throw one out*. Most of the time, the sound of the sentence will guide you.

Original sentence:

>Give <u>him and I</u> the ball.
>Give <u>he and I</u> the ball.

Throw out:

>Give I the ball.
>Give he the ball.

Since you wouldn't say "Give I the ball" or "Give he the ball," you should use the objective "Give him and me the ball."

Note: Do not use reflexive pronouns for subject or object pronouns: *Myself/Himself/Herself/ Ourselves/ Themselves*. Reflexive pronouns are used for the object of a verb when it's the same noun as the subject and are most of the time referring to the same person (e.g., *He accidentally hit himself*).

And then there are the possessive pronouns *my, mine, our, ours, its, his, her, hers, their, theirs, your,* and *yours*, signifying a level of ownership of a given noun.

Many prisoners will attempt to starve <u>themselves</u> to make a point.

This is my book.
This book is mine.
This is our book.
This book is ours.
The dog chased its tail.
The man drove his truck.
That truck is his.
The woman planted her garden.
That garden is hers.
This is their country.
This country is theirs.
This is your land.
This land is yours.

Some say the song "This Land Is <u>Your</u> Land," written by Woodie Guthrie, was originally mocking the song "God Bless America."

AMERICA THE GRAMMAR

A word about writing or announcing your pronouns especially if the pronoun does not match your biological sex.

Except in rare cases, pronouns are used when speaking of someone in the third person. You do not use "he" in the presence of the man you're referring to nor "she" in the presence of the woman you're referring to. You use "you."

If you announce your pronouns that are in line with your biological sex, stop doing this. It's redundant and unnecessary.

More importantly, if you announce your pronouns that are not in line with your biological sex and request or even force another human being to refer to you with the wrong pronoun, it is grammatically incorrect, a form of mind control with roots in communism, and peak narcissism. In addition, you are forcing others to commit the sin of lying. Do not do this.

If you were born a boy, use *he, him,* or *his*. If you were born a girl, use *she, her,* or *hers*.

Prostate (n), Prostrate (v, adj)	*Prostate* (n)—a gland	*Prostate* cancer is easier to beat if you catch it early.
	Prostrate (adj)—a low, submissive, or respectful posture	It is not good for US presidents to *prostrate* themselves in front of foreign leaders.
		Lying *prostrate* is mostly appropriate in church.

Purposefully (adv), Purposely (adv)	*Purposefully* (adv)—with a goal in mind, full of purpose (more purpose than purposely) *Purposely* (adv)—not by accident, with intent	We all should drive *purposely*; it's the driver who can't decide what lane to use that causes most traffic problems. Live *purposefully*; anything less is wasting God's time.
Quotation marks (p)	See also "Punctuation Marks" section. Most of the time, quotation marks (often called quotes) go outside of the punctuation marks. However, that changes when the meaning of what you put in quotes would be altered.	She had me at the word "taco." Did you say, "I don't have a clue"? *This is a question, quoting a statement.* You asked, "Where do you live?" *This is a statement, quoting a question.* I calmly repeated what he yelled at me, "I don't believe you!" *This statement has a different mood than the quote.*
Raise (v), Raze (v)	*Raise* (v)—to lift up or make greater *Raze* (v)—to level to the ground	To *raise* children of high moral character should be the goal of most parents. The independents were willing to *raze* colonial America to the ground in hopes of being free.
Rational (adj), Rationale (n)	*Rational* (adj)—reasonable *Rationale* (n)—reason, justification	The problem with most people on the Left is that they are incapable of *rational* debate. What is the Environmental Protection Agency's *rationale* for virtually ending the coal and oil and gas industries?
Realtor (n)	Often mispronounced real-eh-tor, *realtor* (n) is correct.	Because of the Internet, *realtors* had to rethink how much they charge for their services.
Regretfully (adv), Regrettably (adv)	*Regretfully* (adv)—generally, when a person is full of regret *Regrettably* (adv)—when a situation inspires regret or disappointment	The United States has *regretfully* entered many wars. *Regrettably*, government has become a place for people to get rich off the American taxpayer.

AMERICA THE GRAMMAR

Reluctant (adj), Reticent (adj)	*Reluctant* (adj)—hesitant or unwilling *Reticent* (adj)—is silent or a tendency to be silent	Many people who aren't religious are *reluctant* to become so, mostly because they believe religion makes them give up something. Many non-religious people are *reticent* to discuss religion because of the high emotions this subject elicits.
Repel (v), Repulse (v)	*Repel* (v)—a figurative push back *Repulse* (v)—a physical push back	Her aim was to wear a perfume so pungent that it would *repel* every guy at the concert. The aim of police is to *repulse* unruly protestors.
Reply back (v phrase)	No need for *back*. *Reply* (v) is enough.	Some get offended when you don't *reply* to their texts quickly.
Revert (v), Revert back (v phrase)	*Revert* (v)—go back, return. By adding the word *back*, you're actually going in the original direction.	Let's *revert* to our founding principles and family traditions.
Revolve (v), Rotate (v)	*Revolve* (v)—surrounding an object *Rotate* (v)—an object spinning on its own axis.	The earth not only *revolves* around the sun, but it also *rotates* on its axis.
Root (n, v), Rout (v), Route (n)	*Root* (n) Root—part of a plant or other biological matter, usually underground or below the surface. Figuratively, a deeper part of a whole *Root* (v)—to turn over, dig up, discover *Rout* (v)—to defeat in a big way *Route* (n)—path or course	When we get to the *roots* of a political problems, the issues usually require that we *root* out both the grifters and the cowards who refuse to act. NFL quarterback Tom Brady usually routs most of his opponents. To paraphrase M. Scott Peck, "I took the [route] less traveled by, and that has made all the difference."
Seasons	Do not capitalize the four seasons.	*winter, spring, summer, fall*
Shall (v), Will (v)	When using I or We, *shall* (v) means must, deriving from a sense of responsibility or duty Will (v)—indicating strong odds that something is going to happen	Concealed gun carry laws in many states use the word *shall* issue, meaning that unless the applicant is a convicted felon, the issuing agency must grant the permit. She has a clean record, so she *will* receive her concealed gun permit soon.

Stationary (adj), Stationery (adj)	*Stationary* (adj)—motionless, still *Stationery* (n)—paper to write on, sometimes personalized	Only if you are charged by a grizzly bear should you fall to the ground and remain *stationary*. Otherwise, back away slowly and clear the area. Monogrammed *stationery* makes a nice touch.
Straight (adj), Strait (adj)	*Straight* (adj)—direct line, not crooked *Strait* (n)—smaller body of water that joins two larger bodies of water	If you haven't realized by now, your parents want to keep you on a *straight* path. Life is easier that way. The terrorists in Iran often threaten to close the *Strait* of Hormuz, which connects the Persian Gulf and the Gulf of Oman. This would cut off about twenty percent of the world's oil supply.
Subscribe (v)	*Subscribe* (v)—set up to receive regularly, agree with	I *subscribe* to Walter E. Williams' and Thomas Sowell's points of view, which is why I *subscribe* to their weekly columns.
Subject/verb agreement	Rule: Use singular verbs with singular nouns and plural verbs with plural nouns, and don't let what comes between the nouns and verbs confuse you (bushel of apples). Beware of words like anyone, each (always singular), either, none, and somebody.	Each *signor* of the Declaration of Independence *used his* real signature, publicly daring England to arrest and possibly kill him. The *signors* of the Declaration of Independence risked *their* reputations, fortunes, and freedoms in standing up to England. What if the experiment failed? *None* of the musical artists is from a foreign country. *Either* car *serves* my needs.
Supposably (adv)	*Supposedly* (adv)—presumably, allegedly. Pronunciation is "sup-POH-zed-lee"	America should *supposedly* lead the world in opportunity.

AMERICA THE GRAMMAR

Suppose (v), Supposed to (adj phrase)	*Suppose* (v)—what if *Supposed to* (adj phrase)—obligated	*Suppose* we were to institute a Flat Tax. The economic activity that would follow would be astounding. We are *supposed to* care for others because God, not the government, says so.
Suspect (adj, n), Suspicious (adj)	*Suspect* (adj)—having qualities that make other distrust a person or object, not trustworthy *Suspect* (n)—a person considered to have committed a crime *Suspicious* (adj)—synonym for suspect	If a person becomes a *suspect*, under the Fifth Amendment, he has a right to remain silent and avoid self-incrimination. Be *suspicious* of anyone who says a government program won't cost much or is temporary.
Swam (v), Swum (v)	Today, I *swim* (v). Yesterday, I *swam* (v). Many times, I have *swum* (v). Does *swum* sound funny? Yes. Get over it.	
Taken back (phrase), Taken aback (phrase)	Taken aback—you're frightened or startled. Taken back—you travel in space or time back to a place you have already been.	"The Samaritan woman, *taken aback*, asked, "How come you, a Jew, are asking me, a Samaritan woman, for a drink?" (John 4:9) Mark was *taken back* to his uncle's wedding twenty years ago when he heard that stupid Chicken Dance.
Than (conj, prep), Then (adv)	*Than* (conj)—compares one clause with others *Then* (conj)—joins clauses by time	Why is a baby's life in her mother's womb less important *than* one who has been born? You are a child of God, no less *than* the trees and the stars. First you work, *then* you earn money.

That, Which	Use *that* when what follows is necessary for the meaning of the sentence and *which* when it's not necessary.	On July 9, 1776, there were news reports *that* allegedly caused a riot in New York. The Fourteenth Amendment, *which* was ratified in 1868, addresses citizenship and equal protection under the law.
They're (v phrase), Their (possessive pronoun), There (adv, exclamation)	They are Their (possessive) *There* (adv, exclamation)	By serving their country, US servicemen and women prove their worth; and *they are* supported by grateful Americans. Fourth Amendment: "The right of the people to be secure in *their* persons, houses, papers, and effects, against unreasonable searches and seizures…" *There* is an uncommon way to amend the constitution: A Convention of States. "*There* it is!" she screamed.
Toward (prep), Towards (prep)	*Toward* (prep)—formal *Towards* (prep)—informal	Empires can last many years, but without checks and balances on their power, they creep and sometimes run *toward* extinction.
Use to (incorrect), Used to (v phrase)	When referring to something you may have done in the past, choose *used to*.	We *used to* recite the Pledge of Allegiance every day before school.
Verses (n), Versus (prep)	*Verses* (n)—plural for verse, as in phrases in a book or other piece of writing *Versus* (prep)—as opposed to for matters of comparison	What are your favorite Bible *verses*? In 1973, the Supreme Court ruled mistakenly on the case of Roe *versus* Wade.
Very unique (incorrect adj phrase)	If something is *unique* (adj), it is one of a kind. There is no other. Therefore, there cannot be varying degrees of uniqueness.	The Ocean Dream Diamond is *unique* not for its size but for its color.

AMERICA THE GRAMMAR

Wake (v), woke (v)	*Wake* (v)—rouse yourself or someone else from sleep.	Most people who *wake* early in the day accomplish more. If you *woke* late yesterday, set your alarm for an earlier time.
Warrantee (n), Warranty (n)	*Warrantee* (n)—person whom a warranty is given *Warranty* (n)—contract to fix or repair	Take caution in spending too much money on a *warranty* for electronics; more often than not, they're not necessary.
Wary (adj), Weary (adj)	*Wary* (adj)—suspicious or cautious *Leery* (adj)—synonym for wary *Weary* (adj)—tired, weak	Be *wary/leery* of anyone promising anything free. People who do triathlons don't get *weary* as quickly as others.
Was (v), Were (v)	*If I were* is a subjunctive mood, meaning it expresses a possibility, contingency, or suggestion. Americans increasingly use *If I was*, but it's incorrect.	Federalist Paper #51: "If men *were* angels, no government would be necessary. If angels *were* to govern men, neither external nor internal controls on government would be necessary."
Wet your appetite (phrase)	*Whet your appetite*—sharpen or heighten your appetite—is correct *Wet your whistle*—take a drink—is correct.	Seeing large platters of sushi as we walk into the restaurant *whets our appetite*. Only old people say "*wet your whistle*."
Wiggle (v), Wriggle (v)	*Wiggle* (v)—movement or squirming *Wriggle* (v)—movement away from a current situation or place.	Most perpetrators will *wiggle* in the chair when being questioned. We need to vote for the leader who will not let politicians *wriggle* out of a scandal.
Who, Whom	The rule centers on the predicate nominative, which is a noun or pronoun following a linking verb, and tells us what the subject is. *Who*—subject *Whom*—object The easiest way to determine whether to use *Who* or *Whom* is to swap out another pronoun and place it at the end of the sentence.	

"Who" can be swapped with I, he, she, we, and they.
"Whom" can be swapped with me, him, her, us, and them.

Subject
Who/Whom walked away?
SWAP: He walked away. (Therefore, Who)

Objective
Who/Whom do you trust?
SWAP: I trust him. (Therefore, Whom)

You guys	*Guys* is unnecessary and used too often.	"What can I get *you* (all is implied)?" is a sentence every person should have to ask as a restaurant server.

References

First impressions

Premack, Rachel, and Shana Lebowitz. "Science Says People Decide These 12 Things within Seconds of Meeting You." Business Insider. April 24, 2019. https://www.businessinsider.com/science-of-first-impressions-2015-2.

McAleer, Dr. Phil. "New Research Reveals the Secret to Making a Good First Impression." University of Glasgow. March 14, 2014. https://www.gla.ac.uk/news/archiveofnews/2014/march/headline_312691_en.html.

McAleer, P., Todorov, A., and P. Belin. "How Do You Say 'Hello'?" Personality Impressions from Brief Novel Voices. PLOS ONE, 9(3),e90779. https://journals.plos.org/plosone/article?id=10.1371/journal.pone.0090779.

https://news.softpedia.com/news/First-Impressions-Last-a-Lot-Longer-than-Though-179250.shtml.

Wood, Janice. "The Power of a First Impression." Psych Central. February 15, 2014. https://psychcentral.com/news/2014/02/15/the-power-of-a-first-impression/65944.html.

https://psychcentral.com/news/2011/01/19/first-impressions-are-more-lasting-than-once-thought/22769.html.

Punctuation matters

Garcia, Carlos. "Father-to-Be Killed in Accidental Explosion of Gender-Reveal Device in New York." TheBlaze. February 23, 2021.

https://www.theblaze.com/news/ny-gender-reveal-explosion-death.

Gunner, Jennifer. "What Are the 16 Punctuation Marks in English Grammar?" YourDictionary. October 4, 2022. https://grammar.yourdictionary.com/punctuation/what/fourteen-punctuation-marks.html.

RochesterFirst. 2021. "Dad-to-be killed while putting device together for gender reveal." Updated February 27, 2021. https://www.rochesterfirst.com/news/dad-to-be-killed-while-putting-device-together-for-gender-reveal/.

Wood, Janice. "The Power of a First Impression." Psych Central. February 15, 2014. https://psychcentral.com/news/2014/02/15/the-power-of-a-first-impression/65944.html.

http://news.bbc.co.uk/2/hi/europe/765629.stm.

Definition of grammar

Brians, Paul. 2003. *Common Errors in English Usage*. Oregon: Franklin, Beedle & Associates Inc.

King, Stephen. "Let Your First Draft Rest (Minimum: Six Weeks)." The StephenKing.com Message Board. August 23, 2016. https://stephenking.com/xf/index.php?threads%2Flet-your-first-draft-rest-minimum-six-weeks.3865%2F.

Strunk, William Jr., and White, E. B. *The Elements of Style*.

The Chicago Style Guide.

The AP Style Guide.

http://americanhistory.about.com.

www.archives.gov.

http://bcs.bedfordstmartins.com/smhandbook.

http://biblestudytools.com/bbe/mark/5-30.html.

http://www.dailywritingtips.com/compared-to-or-compared-with/.

http://dictionary.reference.com/.

http://dictionary.reference.com/browse/conscious.

http://www.elearnenglishlanguage.com/difficulties/borrowlendloan.html.

http://www.english.uga.edu/writingcenter/writing/triangle.html.

http://www.farmersalmanac.com/blog/2008/11/17/what-the-pilgrims-really-ate/.
http://grammarist.com/.
http://grammarist.com/usage/cleanup-clean-up/.
http://www.grammar-monster.com.
http://www.history.com/news/9-things-you-may-not-know-about-the-declaration-of-independence.
http://inventors.about.com/od/fstartinventors/ss/Franklin_invent_4.htm.
https://www.keranews.org/texas-news/2014-07-06/how-the-lost-copy-of-the-declaration-of-independence-landed-in-the-dallas-library.
https://languages.oup.com/google-dictionary-en/.
http://www.merriam-webster.com/.
http://www.oed.com/.
https://www.oxfordreference.com/view/10.1093/oi/authority.20111019152836936#:~:text=The%20whole%20system%20and%20structure,of%20the%20seven%20liberal%20arts.
http://www.psychologytoday.com/articles/199401/devastating-difference.
http://www.quickanddirtytips.com/.
http://score.rims.k12.ca.us/score_lessons/women_american_revolution/geiger.html.
https://simple.wikipedia.org/wiki/Grammar.
https://www.vocabulary.com/articles/chooseyourwords/conscious-conscience/.
https://www.vocabulary.com/articles/chooseyourwords/envy-jealousy/.
http://www.vvdailypress.com/articles/battle-36631-bloodiest-soldiers.html.
http://www.washingtonpost.com/lifestyle/kidspost/10-things-you-didnt-know-about-thomas-jefferson/2011/04/12/AGGLlWsH_story.html.
http://www.wsu.edu/~brians/errors/errors.html.

What pilgrims ate

Staff, Farmers' Almanac. "On the Menu: What the Pilgrims Really Ate at Thanksgiving." Farmers' Almanac—Plan Your Day. Grow Your Life. November 9, 2021. https://www.farmersalmanac.com/what-the-pilgrims-really-ate-2197.

Declaration of Independence signed

Harrison, Elizabeth. "9 Things You May Not Know about the Declaration of Independence." History.com. A&E Television Networks. July 4, 2012. https://www.history.com/news/9-things-you-may-not-know-about-the-declaration-of-independence.

Jealousy versus envy

Marano, Hara Estroff. "A Devastating Difference." Psychology Today. Sussex Publishers. January 9, 2016. https://www.psychologytoday.com/intl/articles/199401/devastating-difference.

Thomas Jefferson

"10 Things You Didn't Know about Thomas Jeffersond." The Washington Post. WP Company. June 30, 2011. http://www.washingtonpost.com/lifestyle/kidspost/10-things-you-didnt-know-about-thomas-jefferson/2011/04/12/AGGLlWsH_story.html.

Clean-up hitter

Wood, Robert. "Top 10 Clean-Up Hitters in Baseball." Bleacher Report. Bleacher Report, October 2, 2017. https://bleacherreport.com/articles/1612071-top-10-clean-up-hitters-in-baseball.

Slaves to America

Borucki, Alex. "Trans-Atlantic Slave Trade—Estimates." Slave Voyages. Multiple Universities. Accessed April 12, 2023. https://www.slavevoyages.org/assessment/estimates.
Gates, Henry Louis. "How Many Slaves Landed in the US?" PBS. Public Broadcasting Service, September 19, 2013. https://www.pbs.org/wnet/african-americans-many-rivers-to-cross/history/how-many-slaves-landed-in-the-us/.

Lincoln assassinated at premiere of Our American Cousin

Klein, Christopher. "10 Things You May Not Know about the Lincoln Assassination." History.com. A&E Television Networks. November 8, 2021. https://www.history.com/news/10-things-you-may-not-know-about-the-lincoln-assassination.
https://forum-theatre.com/when-was-lincoln-shot-at-the-fodl-theatre/.

This Land Is Your Land

https://www.songmeaningsandfacts.com/this-land-is-your-land/.

About the Author

M. A. Cummings has a bachelor's degree in business management from St. John's University in Collegeville, Minnesota, and a master's degree in rhetoric and composition from Northern Arizona University in Flagstaff, Arizona. In addition to a wealth of marketing and sales collateral, he has written a weekly column for two university newspapers, a grammar column, and movie review for a 1,500-employee corporation and served as a regular columnist for www.clashdaily.com and www.dailysurge.com. He has also written position pieces for the 2010 Trevor Drown for the US Senate (AR) and 2012 Joe Coors for Congress (CO) campaigns.

Cummings lives with his wife, children, and dogs in Colorado.

Printed in the USA
CPSIA information can be obtained
at www.ICGtesting.com
LVHW021958020324
773348LV00007B/324